A WEALTH OF WISDOM

❖ ❖ ❖

MICHAEL LYNBERG

ST. MARTIN'S GRIFFIN
NEW YORK

A WEALTH OF WISDOM

❖ ❖ ❖

620 WORLD PROVERBS FOR
CONTENTMENT AND PROSPERITY

Book design by Gretchen Achilles

ISBN 0-312-14392-3

First St. Martin's Griffin Edition: June 1996

10   9   8   7   6   5   4   3   2   1

FOR ELIZABETH

PREFACE

Aristotle collected them. Shakespeare used them in his plays. Winston Churchill found them to be a powerful rhetorical device, as did Lincoln, Kennedy, and many other leaders. Diplomats and businesspeople, through the ages, have used them to cross cultural barriers and to make a point concisely and dramatically.

Proverbs have been called "the children of truth," "the coins of the people," and "the wisdom of many, the wit of one." They are, as Cervantes remarked, "short sentences drawn from long experience," and they are part of the rich cultural heritage of every nation in the world.

Many proverbs relate to business and trade since these have long been part of the human experience and since the scope of business is as broad as life itself. Many offer wise advice on sales, marketing, management, and finance, while others offer timeless insights on human relations and other areas of personal development vital to success.

The French believe that "a proverb is to speech what salt is to food." The Chinese say, "When one has read a book of proverbs, no effort is needed to speak well." Russians remark that "a proverb is always wise," and the Spanish point out that "a person's life is often built on a proverb." It is my hope that the proverbs in this brief collection will prove entertaining to read, worthwhile to remember, and practical to use.

MICHAEL LYNBERG
CAMBRIDGE, MASSACHUSETTS

A bad workman quarrels with his tools.

ENGLISH

A bad year has thirteen months.

GREEK

A boat doesn't go forward if each is rowing his own way.

AFRICAN (SWAHILI)

A broken hand works, but not a broken heart.

PERSIAN

A change of work is as good as rest.

IRISH

A clean mouth and an honest hand will take a man through any land.

GERMAN

A clear conscience is a good pillow.

FRENCH

A clever person turns great troubles into little ones, and little ones into none at all.

CHINESE

A closed mouth catches no flies.

ENGLISH

A concentrated mind will pierce a rock.

JAPANESE

A crown is no cure for a headache.

YIDDISH

A dog is a lion in his own house.

PERSIAN

A fair character is a fair fortune.

IRISH

A fine horse runs by observing the shadows of the whip.

JAPANESE

A fool and his money are soon parted.

ENGLISH

A fool is busy in everyone's business but his own.

ENGLISH

A friend who is made in a year may be lost in an hour.

CHINESE

A gem is not polished without friction, nor a person perfected
without trials.

CHINESE

A good character is the real beauty that never fades.

PHILIPPINE

A good example is the best sermon.

ENGLISH

A good reputation is worth every sacrifice.

KURDISH

A good seaman is known in bad weather.

ITALIAN

A guest sees more in an hour than the host in a year.

POLISH

A hundred years cannot repair a moment's loss of honor.

ITALIAN

A journey of a thousand miles begins with a single step.

CHINESE

A late man brings trouble on himself.

IRISH

A lawyer's opinion is worth nothing unless it is paid for.

ENGLISH

A lazy shepherd is the wolf's friend.

WELSH

A liar's punishment: he is not believed when telling the truth.

ITALIAN

A lie travels around the world while the truth is putting
on her shoes.

FRENCH

A little impatience will spoil great plans.

CHINESE

A man does not live a hundred years, yet he worries enough
for a thousand.

CHINESE

A man without a smiling face should not open shop.

CHINESE

A man without money is like a ship without sails.

JAPANESE

A mule laden with gold is welcome at every castle.

ARMENIAN

A noisy dog is not fit for hunting.

INDIAN (TAMIL)

A peasant between two lawyers is like a fish between two cats.

SPANISH

A PLANT, OFTEN TRANSPLANTED, NEVER PROSPERS.

LATIN

A servant is known in the absence of his master.

ENGLISH

A skillful trade is better than an inherited fortune.

WELSH

A small leak will sink a great ship.

RUSSIAN

A soft answer turns away wrath.

DUTCH

A statement once let loose cannot be caught by four horses.

JAPANESE

A steady occupation keeps one away from mischief.

SPANISH

A stumble may prevent a fall.

ENGLISH

A turtle travels only when it sticks its neck out.

KOREAN

A wildflower on the mountaintop would not change places
with a rose in the garden.

ARMENIAN

A wise man changes his mind; a fool, never.

SPANISH

A wolf may grow old and gray but his mind doesn't change
until his dying day.

GREEK

Ability and necessity dwell in the same cabin.

DUTCH

Accusing the times is but excusing ourselves.

ENGLISH

After one who earns comes one who wastes.

DANISH

After three days, both fish and guests begin to smell.

DANISH

Aim high in your career, but stay humble in your heart.

KOREAN

All locks open with a golden key.

YIDDISH

All things are difficult before they are easy.

ENGLISH

Always leave a way of escape to the erring.

CHINESE

An hour of play discovers more than a year of conversation.

PORTUGUESE

An hour will destroy what it took an age to build.

ENGLISH

An inch to the eye of a servant is a foot to the eye of his master.

JAPANESE

An income is what you can't live within or without.

AMERICAN

An old error has more friends than a new truth.

GERMAN

An open door may tempt a saint.

SPANISH

Anger makes a fool out of the wise.

YIDDISH

Anger punishes itself.

ENGLISH

As is the king, so are his people.

SPANISH

As long as you live, keep learning how to live.

LATIN

As the wallet grows, so do the needs.

YIDDISH

Ask the young, they know everything.

FRENCH

Assist him who is carrying his burden, but by no means him
who is laying it aside.

LATIN

At a good bargain pause and ponder.

ITALIAN

Bargain like a gypsy, but pay like a gentleman.

HUNGARIAN

Be always a little bit afraid so that you never have need of being much afraid.

FRENCH

Be an old man when you are young, so you can be a young boy in your old age.

CZECH

Be it better, be it worse, be ruled by him who has the purse.

IRISH

Be not afraid of going slowly; be afraid of standing still.

JAPANESE

Be silent, or say something better than silence.

GERMAN

Be willing to start with a low position if you wish to attain
a high one.

JAPANESE

BEFORE YOU GO, THINK OF YOUR RETURN.

BOSNIAN

Begin with an error of an inch, and end by being a thousand miles off the mark.

CHINESE

Behave toward everyone as if receiving a guest.

CHINESE

Being without money is always a mistake.

YIDDISH

Being young is a fault which diminishes daily.

SWEDISH

Better a friend's bite than an enemy's caress.

DANISH

Better a hundred enemies outside the house than one inside.

ARABIAN

Better a slip of the foot than a slip of the tongue.

SPANISH

Better a steady dime than a rare dollar.

YIDDISH

Better an ass that carries you than a horse that throws you.

ITALIAN

Better poor with honor than rich with shame.

DUTCH

Better to ask your way than go astray.

ENGLISH

Better to die standing than to live on your knees.

YIDDISH

Beware of him who regards not his reputation.

ENGLISH

Beware of the person with nothing to lose.

ITALIAN

Boasting begins where wisdom stops.

JAPANESE

Boldness takes cities.

RUSSIAN

Books are nourishment to the mind.

ITALIAN

Bravery is the fruit of a thousand hardships.

PHILIPPINE

Burnt with the hot, you blow on the cold.

YIDDISH

Business neglected is business lost.

"But" is a fence over which few leap.

By asking for the impossible, we obtain the best possible.

By labor is fire got out of stone.

By year's end, the servant has acquired the bad habits of his master.

Carelessness is a great enemy.

JAPANESE

Change yourself and your fortune will change.

PORTUGUESE

Cheerful company shortens the miles.

GERMAN

Choose a job you love, and you'll never have to work
a day in your life.

CHINESE

Common sense is not so common.

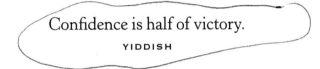

Confidence is half of victory.

Consider the servants and you will know the master.

Consult your purse before you buy.

Courage is the best defense.

Courtesy wins friends.

RUSSIAN

Deal with the faults of others as gently as with your own.

CHINESE

Difficulties give way to diligence.

ENGLISH

Dig a well before you are thirsty.

FRENCH

Discretion is the better part of valor.

ENGLISH

Don't be too sweet or you'll be eaten up; too bitter, or you'll be spat out.

YIDDISH

Don't bite off more than you can chew.

AMERICAN

Don't jump high in a low-ceilinged room.

CZECH

Don't leave the high road for a shortcut.

PORTUGUESE

DON'T LET GRASS GROW ON THE PATH OF FRIENDSHIP.

NATIVE AMERICAN

Don't neglect your own field to plow your neighbor's.

ENGLISH

Don't postpone a good deed.

IRISH

Don't pour away the water you are traveling with because of a mirage.

ARABIAN

Don't protect yourself by a fence, but by your friends.

CZECH

Don't put your affairs into the hands of someone who has failed to manage his own.

MALTESE

Don't rely on the label on the bag.

FRENCH

Don't sell the skin until you have caught the bear.

ENGLISH

Don't suppose that you know a man until you come to divide a spoil with him.

IRISH

Don't tell secrets in front of servants.

ARABIAN

Don't think there are no crocodiles because the water is calm.

MALAYSIAN

Does your neighbor bore you? Lend him some money.

ITALIAN

Doubt, and you'll not be deceived.

FRENCH

Drive your business, that it not drive you.

AMERICAN

Drown not yourself to save a drowning man.

ENGLISH

Eagles fly alone.

ENGLISH

Envy shoots at others and wounds itself.

ENGLISH

Even if the stream is shallow, wade it as if it were deep.

KOREAN

Even the highest tower begins from the ground.

CHINESE

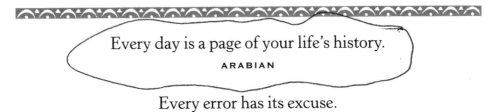

Every day is a page of your life's history.

ARABIAN

Every error has its excuse.

POLISH

Every fish that gets away appears great.

TURKISH

Every village has its village idiot.

YIDDISH

Every way up has its way down.

YIDDISH

Everybody knows good advice except him who needs it.

GERMAN

Everybody's responsibility is nobody's responsibility.

ENGLISH

Everyone can navigate in fine weather.

ITALIAN

Everyone gives a push to the house that is about to fall.

SWISS

Everything new meets resistance.

RUSSIAN

Experience is not bound to years, for years may be lived
in a single hour.

SWISS

Experience is the comb that nature gives us when we are bald.

CHINESE

Failures are the pillars of success.

WELSH

Failure teaches you more than success.

RUSSIAN

Fame is but the breath of the people.

Fire in the heart sends smoke into the head.

First deserve, then desire.

Fish see the bait but not the hook; men see the profit but
not the peril.

For the diligent, the week has seven days; for the lazy, seven tomorrows.

GERMAN

For the disease of stubbornness there is no cure.

YIDDISH

Fortune favors the bold.

SPANISH

Fortune has weak hands, for whom she lifts up she soon lets fall.

GERMAN

FORTUNE IS A WOMAN: IF YOU NEGLECT HER TODAY, DON'T EXPECT TO GET HER BACK TOMORROW.

FRENCH

Fortune sells what we think she gives.

FRENCH

From a little spark may burst a mighty flame.

LATIN

From small beginnings come great things.

DUTCH

Genius is one part inspiration and three parts perspiration.

AMERICAN

Getting money is like digging with a needle; spending money
is like water soaking into sand.

JAPANESE

Gifts can soften even stone.

PHILIPPINE

Give a man a fish, and you feed him for a day; teach a man
to fish, and you feed him for a lifetime.

CHINESE

Give an egg to a greedy person and he'll ask for the hen.

SPANISH

Give neither advice nor salt until you are asked for it.

ENGLISH

Go and wake up your luck!

PERSIAN

Go to a man who is in difficulty and you'll get a bargain.

IRISH

God gave us two ears and one mouth that we use them in the same proportion.

IRISH

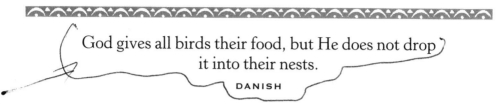

God gives all birds their food, but He does not drop it into their nests.

DANISH

God helps the poor: He protects them from expensive sins.

YIDDISH

God respects me when I work, and loves me when I sing.

THAI

Gold dust blinds all eyes.

ENGLISH

Gold glitters in the mud.

YIDDISH

Good bargains empty the purse.

ITALIAN

Good wares make a quick market.

SCOTTISH

Grain by grain, a loaf; stone by stone, a castle.

BULGARIAN

Grasp no more than thy hand will hold.

ENGLISH

Great fortunes depend on luck; small fortunes depend on diligence.

Great men's requests are commands.

Habits are at first cobwebs; at last, chains.

Haste and careful work never go together.

Hasty climbers have sudden falls.

He buys honey too dear, who licks it from thorns.

FRENCH

He can who believes he can.

LATIN

He does a good day's work who rids himself of a fool.

FRENCH

He has good judgment who does not rely solely on his own.

ENGLISH

He has the greatest blind side who thinks he has none.

DUTCH

He is a giant who is surrounded by dwarfs.

YIDDISH

He is not worth hiring who talks of tiring.

ENGLISH

He is wise who can make a friend of a foe.

SCOTTISH

He labors in vain who tries to please everybody.

LATIN

He who begins much, finishes little.

GERMAN

He who builds according to everyone's advice will have
a crooked house.

DANISH

He who buys what he doesn't need must often sell what
he does need.

ENGLISH

He who conquers his anger has conquered an enemy.

GERMAN

He who doesn't keep his own secret won't keep another's.

SPANISH

HE WHO DOES NOT MIX WITH THE CROWD KNOWS NOTHING.

SPANISH

He who falls with honor soon gets to his feet again.

GERMAN

He who fears to suffer, suffers from fear.

FRENCH

He who is afraid of asking is afraid of learning.

DANISH

He who is free of faults will never die.

AFRICAN (CONGO)

He who is good for making excuses is seldom good
for anything else.

AMERICAN

He who is his own lawyer has a fool for a client.

ENGLISH

He who is shut outside is forgotten inside.

FRENCH

He who is timid in asking gives courage to refuse.

GERMAN

He who laughs, lasts.

NORWEGIAN

He who likes things to be easy will have difficulties: he who likes problems will succeed.

LAOTIANS

He who lives well is learned enough.

ENGLISH

He who pays the piper calls the tune.

ENGLISH

He who places his ladder too steeply easily falls backward.

CZECH

He who steals a needle will steal an ox.

KOREAN

He who threatens is afraid.

FRENCH

He who wants the kernel must crack the nut.

GERMAN

He who won't be advised, can't be helped.

GERMAN

He who would gather honey must brave the stinging of the bees.

LEBANESE

He who would leap high must take a long run.

DANISH

He who would stand up in the world must first learn to stoop.

JAPANESE

Hens that cackle much lay few eggs.

ESTONIAN

Heroism consists of hanging on one minute longer.

NORWEGIAN

Honesty makes rich, but she works slowly.

GERMAN

Honor is better than honors.

BELGIAN

Honey on his tongue—guard your purse!

GERMAN

Hope for the best and prepare for the worst.

ENGLISH

How beautiful it is to do nothing, and then to rest afterward.

SPANISH

However much you eat, leave some seed for sowing.

LATVIA

I am a gentleman, you are a gentleman; who is going to mind the swine?

CZECH

If and *When* were planted and *Nothing* grew.

TURKISH

If at first you don't succeed, try, try again.

ENGLISH

If better were within, better would come out.

If it doesn't get better, depend on it, it will get worse.

If one horse runs wild, the rest of the flock will follow suit.

If small sums do not go out, large sums will not come in.

If the family lives in harmony, all affairs will prosper.

If the rich could hire other people to die for them, the poor would make a wonderful living.

If thine enemy falls beneath thy foot, crush him.

If two people keep a horse, it will be thin; if two people share a boat, it will leak.

If you act like an ass, don't get insulted if people ride you.

IF YOU ARE AFRAID
OF GETTING WET, YOU
WILL NEVER MAKE
A GOOD FISHERMAN.

ARMENIAN

If you are healthy, you're wealthy.

YIDDISH

If you are patient in one moment of anger, you will escape
a hundred days of sorrow.

CHINESE

If you are skilled, your wallet will be filled.

YIDDISH

If you are standing upright, do not fear a crooked shadow.

CHINESE

If you can—do!

YIDDISH

If you buy cheap meat, when it boils you smell what you have saved.

ARABIAN

If you call one wolf, you invite the pack.

BULGARIAN

If you can't bite, don't show your teeth.

YIDDISH

If you can't do as you wish, do as you can.

SPANISH

If you don't have a plan for yourself, you will be part
of someone else's.

AMERICAN

If you have money, you are wise and good looking and
can sing well, too.

YIDDISH

If you pay the laborer in advance, you have to gather
your own harvest.

RUSSIAN

If you pay with peanuts, expect to get monkeys.

AMERICAN

If you run after luck, you will spoil many pairs of shoes.

RUSSIAN

If you run after two rabbits, you won't catch either one.

ARMENIAN

If you sow hope, you reap love.

RUSSIAN

If you take big paces, you leave big spaces.

BURMESE

If you tell your secret to your servant, you have made him
your master.

SCOTTISH

If you cleanse others, like soap you will waste away in the process.

AFRICAN (MADAGASCAR)

If you understand everything, you must be misinformed.

JAPANESE

If you walk straight, you will not stumble.

YIDDISH

If you want good service, serve yourself.

SPANISH

If you want to be strong, know your weaknesses.

GERMAN

If you want to succeed, first help others to succeed.

JAPANESE

If you wish to know what a man is, place him in authority.

CZECH

If you work in the heat, you will have something to eat in the cold.

RUSSIAN

If you would be rich in a year, you may be hanged in six months.

ITALIAN

If you would know the value of money, go and try to borrow some.

AMERICAN

If you would not be cheated, ask the price at three shops.

CHINESE

If you would take, first give.

JAPANESE

If youth knew what age would crave, it would both get and save.

ENGLISH

Ill-matched horses draw badly.

DANISH

In a calm sea, every man is a pilot.

SPANISH

Ingratitude sickens benevolence.

GERMAN

Insult begets insult.

GREEK

In strategy, secrecy is esteemed.

JAPANESE

In the land of promise, a man may die of hunger.

DANISH

In unity, little things increase; in discord, big things decrease.

GERMAN

It is a bad hen that eats at your house and lays at another's.

SPANISH

It is a bad plan that admits of no modification.

LATIN

It is a foolish sheep that makes the wolf its confessor.

ITALIAN

IT IS A ROUGH ROAD
THAT LEADS TO THE HEIGHTS
OF GREATNESS.

LATIN

It's best to save at the top of the sack.

SWEDISH

It is better to be loved than feared.

AFRICAN (SENEGAL)

It is better to go to bed on an empty stomach than to rise with debts.

LATVIA

It is better to profit selling dirt than to lose selling musk.

ARABIAN

It is better to light a candle than to curse the darkness.

CHINESE

It is better to suffer for truth than to prosper by falsehood.

DANISH

It is difficult to trap an old fox.

DANISH

It is easy to go from economy to extravagance; it is hard to go from extravagance to economy.

CHINESE

It is good fishing in troubled waters.

DUTCH

It is harder to lift the arm than the tongue.

RUSSIAN

It is pleasant to command, be it only a herd of cattle.

SPANISH

It is only at the tree loaded with fruit that the people throw stones.

FRENCH

It is the pace that kills.

ENGLISH

It is usually the reply that causes the fight.

JAPANESE

Judge not the ship as she lies on the docks.

ITALIAN

Keep bad men company and you'll soon be of their number.

ENGLISH

Keep thy shop and thy shop will keep thee.

ENGLISH

Keep your friends close, but keep your enemies closer.

SICILIAN

Kill the elk in your youth if you would lie on its skin in your old age.

FINNISH

Kill the spider and you will destroy the cobweb.

MALTESE

Kindness begets kindness.

SWEDISH

Large fish do not live in small ponds.

JAPANESE

Laziness goes so slowly that poverty overtakes it.

DUTCH

Learning is a treasure which follows its owner everywhere.

CHINESE

Learning is like rowing against the stream: if one does not advance, one falls back.

CHINESE

Let not your tongue cut your throat.

ARABIAN

Life is a long journey taken with heavy packs on one's back.

JAPANESE

Life is an onion which one peels crying.

FRENCH

Life is like a bubble that may vanish at any time.

PHILIPPINE

Life is partly what we make it, and partly what it is made
by the friends whom we choose.

CHINESE

Light gains make heavy purses.

SPANISH

Little by little one walks far.

PERUVIAN

Little is done where many command.

DUTCH

Little is spent with difficulty, much with ease.

CHINESE

Live within your harvest.

PERSIAN

Lose an hour in the morning and you'll be running after it all day.

ENGLISH

Loyalty is more valuable than diamonds.

PHILIPPINE

Luck is the idol of the idle.

ENGLISH

Luck is where preparation meets opportunity.

AMERICAN

Make no promises when you are seized by joy; write no letters
when you are seized by anger.

CHINESE

Make sure to be in with your equals if you're going to fall out
with your superiors.

YIDDISH

MAKING A SHOW OF ONESELF
IS A NECESSARY ART
OF LIVING.

JAPANESE

Many a shabby colt makes a fine horse.

IRISH

Many hands make light work.

ENGLISH

Many things are lost for want of asking.

ENGLISH

Master easy, servant slack.

CHINESE

Masters should sometimes be blind, sometimes deaf.

ENGLISH

Mediocrity is climbing molehills without sweating.

ICELANDIC

Men in the game are often blind to what men looking on see clearly.

CHINESE

Misfortune comes on horseback and goes away on foot.

FRENCH

Misfortune does not come with a bell on its neck.

ESTONIAN

Moderate riches will carry you; if you have more,
you must carry them.

ENGLISH

Money goes to money.

YIDDISH

Money grows on the tree of patience.

JAPANESE

Money is the best soap—it can remove the biggest of stains.

YIDDISH

Money loves to be counted.

Money often costs too much.

Money swore an oath that nobody who didn't love
it should ever have it.

More precious than gold are the adversities of youth.

Necessity is the mother of invention.

RUSSIAN

Necessity never made a good bargain.

AMERICAN

Neither sign a paper without reading it, nor drink
water without seeing it.

SPANISH

Never get in a spraying contest with a skunk.

AMERICAN

New day, new fate.

BULGARIAN

No man is good unless others are made better by him.

WELSH

Never make troubles of trifles.

ENGLISH

Never spur a willing horse.

ENGLISH

No help is also sometimes help.

GERMAN

No matter how far you have traveled on the wrong road, turn back.

TURKISH

No mountain is so high that an ass loaded with gold cannot climb it.

SPANISH

No one is so active as a lazy man when he sets out to work.

BELGIAN

No one knows less than he who knows it all.

WELSH

No sweet without sweat.

ENGLISH

Nothing is so certain as the unexpected.

ENGLISH

Nothing seems expensive on credit.

CZECH

Nothing succeeds like success.

ENGLISH

Nothing ventured, nothing gained.

ENGLISH

Of all crafts, to make yourself an honest person is the greatest.

ENGLISH

Of saving comes having.

ENGLISH

Old praise dies unless you feed it.

ENGLISH

One accident teaches us more than a thousand good counsels.

TURKISH

One bag of money is stronger than two bags of truth.

DANISH

One cannot jump higher than one's head.

FINNISH

ONE CHOPS THE WOOD, THE OTHER DOES THE GRUNTING.

YIDDISH

One enemy is too many, and a hundred friends are too few.

ICELANDIC

One eye of the master sees more than ten of the servants.

ENGLISH

One falsehood spoils a thousand truths.

AFRICAN (SWAHILI)

One good head is better than a great many hands.

ENGLISH

One lawyer will make work for another.

SPANISH

One lie draws ten after it.

YIDDISH

One person tells a falsehood and a hundred repeat it as true.

CHINESE

One must scratch people where they itch.

FRENCH

One must step back to make a better leap.

FRENCH

One of these days is none of these days.

ENGLISH

One pretty woman can turn many wise men into fools.

RUSSIAN

One should build as if one were to live forever, and live as
if one were to die tomorrow.

GERMAN

One should not employ those one suspects, nor suspect
those one employs.

FRENCH

One speck of rat dung ruins the whole pot of rice.

CHINESE

One sprinkles the most sugar where the tart is burnt.

DUTCH

One sword keeps another in its sheath.

ENGLISH

One "Take this" is better than two "Thou shalt haves."

FRENCH

One who grabs too much may lose it all.

SWEDISH

One who throws mud gets himself soiled as well.

AFRICAN (SWAHILI)

Open not your sail to every wind.

CHINESE

Our debts eat with us from one dish.

CZECH

Our last garment is made with no pockets.

ITALIAN

Our luxuries are always masquerading as necessities.

AMERICAN

Pain is the price that God puts on all things.

ENGLISH

Pardon one offense and you encourage the commission of many.

LATIN

Pardoning the bad is injuring the good.

ENGLISH

Patience is bitter, but its fruit is sweet.

JAPANESE

Patience wears away stones.

ENGLISH

People count up the faults of those who keep them waiting.

FRENCH

Plan your work and work your plan.

Pleasure is shallow, trouble deep.

Plow deep while others sleep and you shall have corn
to sell and keep.

Praise loudly, blame softly.

Praise the ripe field and not the green corn.

IRISH

Praise without profits puts little into the pot.

ENGLISH

Pray to God, but continue to row toward shore.

RUSSIAN

Prepaid work has lead in its feet.

GERMAN

Pride goes before the fall.

ENGLISH

Pride went out on horseback and returned on foot.

ITALIAN

Procrastination is the thief of time.

ENGLISH

Promises made at sea are often not kept on land.

RUSSIAN

Prosperity makes friends, adversity tries them.

LATIN

Prudent pauses forward business.

ENGLISH

PUT OFF FOR ONE DAY AND TEN DAYS WILL PASS.

KOREAN

Ready money works great cures.

Reckon loss before you reckon gain.

Revenge is a dish that should be eaten cold.

Rivalry is a blessing to men.

Rotten wood cannot be carved.

Row with the oars you have.

DUTCH

Rule your passions or they will rule you.

GREEK

Save money and money will save you.

JAMAICAN

Secrecy is the soul of business.

SPANISH

Seek counsel from him who makes you weep, and not
from him who makes you laugh.

ARABIAN

Self-assurance is two-thirds of success.

IRISH

Settle one difficulty and you keep a hundred others away.

CHINESE

Shared joy is double joy; shared sorrow is half-sorrow.

SWEDISH

Ships are mostly shipwrecked near the shore.

ENGLISH

Short debts make long friends.

ENGLISH

Skill and confidence are an unconquered army.

ENGLISH

Slow and steady wins the race.

ENGLISH

Smoke does not make the pot boil.

TURKISH

Something is learned every time a book is opened.

CHINESE

Speech is the picture of the mind.

SCOTTISH

Spending is quick, earning is slow.

RUSSIAN

Spread a rumor and someone else's lie may become your own.

JAPANESE

Start talking about someone and instantly his shadow appears.

JAPANESE

Stay awhile and lose a mile.

DUTCH

Strength is defeated by strategy.

PHILIPPINE

Take a leap with a sword in your teeth!

KOREAN

Take care of the minutes and the hours will take care of themselves.

AMERICAN

Take fortune by the forelock, for it is bald behind.

ENGLISH

Tell me and I'll forget; show me and I may remember; involve me and I'll understand.

CHINESE

That is a wise delay which makes the road safe.

SPANISH

The art is not in making money, but in keeping it.

DUTCH

The best mirror is an old friend.

SPANISH

The best passion is compassion.

JAMAICAN

The best wealth is health.

WELSH

The borrower is the servant of the lender.

FRENCH

The buyer needs a hundred eyes, the seller but one.

ITALIAN

The devil tempts the busy man, but the idle man tempts the devil.

TURKISH

The door of success is marked *Push* and *Pull*.

YIDDISH

The emptier the kettle, the louder the noise.

RUSSIAN

The friend who can be bought is not worth buying.

IRISH

The friends of my friends are my friends.

BELGIAN

The future belongs to him who knows how to wait.

RUSSIAN

THE HAND THAT WILL
HELP YOU IS OFTEN AT
THE END OF YOUR
OWN SLEEVE.

AMERICAN

The golden age was never the present age.

The great man is he who does not lose his child's heart.

The future is purchased by the present.

The hardest work is to be idle.

The heaviest burden is an empty pocket.

The higher the monkey climbs, the more he shows his bald behind.

FRENCH

The higher the rise, the greater the fall.

FRENCH

The idler will always find company.

ESTONIAN

The last seven hairs are combed with special care.

RUSSIAN

The lawyer's ink writes nothing until you have thrown silver into it.

ESTONIAN

The lion that moves silently is the one that eats the meat.

AFRICAN (SWAHILI)

The man who moved a mountain was he who began
carrying away the small stones.

CHINESE

The mistakes of others are good teachers.

ESTONIAN

The most wasted of all days is the day when we have not laughed.

FRENCH

The night rinses what the day has soaped.

SWISS

The only way to begin on top is to dig a hole.

AMERICAN

The plow that works is always shiny.

GREEK

The real fault is not abandoning a fault.

CHINESE

The reputation of a thousand years may be determined
by the conduct of a single hour.

JAPANESE

The richest man, whatever his lot, is he who's content
with what he's got.

DUTCH

The silent person is often worth listening to.

JAPANESE

The smoothest way is full of stones.

YIDDISH

The stable wears out the horse more than the road.

FRENCH

The steps of the master enrich the field.

FINNISH

The timid person loses many good things.

GREEK

The tree of wisdom is watered by tears.

SWISS

The truth may walk around naked; a lie has to be clothed.

YIDDISH

The way to be safe is to never be secure.

ENGLISH

The winter asks what the summer has earned.

GERMAN

The wise man doesn't tell what he does, and never does what cannot be told.

CHINESE

The wise man is great in small things; the petty man is small in great things.

CHINESE

The wise man weighs his words on the goldsmith's scale.

GERMAN

The wise seek wisdom; the fool has found it.

RUSSIAN

The wolf will hire himself out very cheaply as a shepherd.

RUSSIAN

The world is a sure teacher, but it requires a fat fee.

FINNISH

The world wishes to be deceived.

LATIN

The worst wheel makes the most noise.

DUTCH

The would-be buyer always depreciates.

ITALIAN

There are no traffic jams when you go the extra mile.

AMERICAN

There is a piece of fortune in misfortune.

JAPANESE

There is no hell like a troubled conscience.

ENGLISH

THERE IS NO PROSPERITY
WITHOUT ADVERSITY.

WELSH

There is no time like the present.

ENGLISH

There is no worse counselor than fear.

CHILEAN

There is nothing more shrewd than to pretend to be stupid.

SPANISH

They who in quarrels interpose, will often be wiping a bloody nose.

ENGLISH

Thieves also have principles.

CHINESE

Think before you speak and look before you leap.

IRISH

Think twice before accepting honey that is offered on a sharp knife.

TIBETAN

Those to whom you owe large sums should be visited regularly.

CHINESE

Those who can't dance say the music is no good.

JAMAICAN

Those who have free seats at the theater are the first to hiss.

CHINESE

Though the snake be small, hit it with a big stick.

INDIAN (TAMIL)

Though the thorn in your foot be small, stop and take it out.

INDIAN (HINDI)

Though thine enemy seems like a mouse, watch him like a lion.

ITALIAN

Thought unassisted by learning is perilous.

CHINESE

To a leaking ship every wind is foul.

ITALIAN

To believe a thing impossible is to make it so.

FRENCH

To do, one must be doing.

FRENCH

To know the road ahead, ask those coming back.

CHINESE

To know the value of money, go and try to borrow some.

AMERICAN

To lose your way is one way of finding it.

AFRICAN (SWAHILI)

To open a shop is easy, to keep it open is an art.

To respond immediately to an angry person is like throwing
fuel on a fire.

To succeed, consult three old people.

To whom you tell your secret, to him you resign your liberty.

Tomorrow is often the busiest day of the week.

SPANISH

Too many captains run the ship aground.

GREEK

Too much consulting confounds.

ENGLISH

Too many cousins ruin the shopkeeper.

JAMAICAN

Too much modesty is half conceit.

YIDDISH

Travel ripens a man.

PERSIAN

Trouble is like strong medicine: too much at a time is harmful.

YIDDISH

Truth and oil always come to the surface.

SPANISH

Try before you trust.

ENGLISH

Turn your tongue seven times before speaking.

FRENCH

Two things never to be angry about: what you can help
and what you cannot.

SCOTTISH

Under a flowering bush sometimes lurks a snake.

SPANISH

Under white ashes often lie golden embers.

DANISH

Union is strength.

DUTCH

Unity among the cattle makes the lion lie down hungry.

AFRICAN (SWAHILI)

Unwilling service earns no thanks.

DANISH

Uphill one climbs slowly; downhill one rolls fast.

YIDDISH

Use soft words and hard arguments.

ENGLISH

Useless laws diminish the authority of necessary ones.

FRENCH

VENTURE A SMALL FISH TO CATCH A GREAT ONE.

ENGLISH

Victory has a hundred fathers, defeat is an orphan.

CHINESE

Vows made in storms are forgotten in calms.

ENGLISH

Walk fast and you catch misfortune; walk slowly and it catches you.

JAPANESE

Walls have ears; bottles, mouths.

JAPANESE

Warm up a frozen snake and he will bite you.

ARMENIAN

We confess small faults in order to insinuate that
we don't have great ones.

FRENCH

We make a living by what we get; we make a life by what we give.

AMERICAN

Wealth is like manure: it's useful only when spread around.

CHINESE

Weep once when things are expensive; weep often
when they are cheap.

INDIAN (HINDI)

Well done is better than well said.

FRENCH

Were his word a bridge, it would be risky to pass over it.

YIDDISH

What is the use of a silver cup if it is full of tears?

YIDDISH

What is told in a man's ear is often heard a hundred miles away.

CHINESE

What may be done at any time will be done at no time.

ENGLISH

When a king makes a mistake, all the people suffer.

CHINESE

When a man is happy, he does not hear the clock strike.

GERMAN

When a thief kisses you, count your teeth.

YIDDISH

When anger speaks, wisdom veils her face.

CHINESE

When doing good works, let no one best you.

CHINESE

When going to bed, leave your troubles in your shoes.

DUTCH

When men come face-to-face, their differences vanish.

CHINESE

When one must, one can.

YIDDISH

When there are no fish in one spot, cast your net in another.

CHINESE

When the cart breaks down, advice is plentiful.

ARMENIAN

When the game is over, the king goes back in the sack
just like the pawn.

ITALIAN

When the ship is sunk, everyone knows how she
could have been saved.

ITALIAN

When two dogs fight for a bone, a third runs away with it.

DUTCH

When you are losing, wear a winning face.

FRENCH

When you go out to buy, don't show your silver.

When you go out to buy, use your eyes and not your ears.

When you go to your neighbor's, you find out what
is happening at home.

When you have money, think of the time when you had none.

When you look to the heights, hold on to your hat.

YIDDISH

Who is once found to be bad is presumed to be so forever.

LATIN

Where nettles flourish, roses don't.

RUSSIAN

Where there was a skunk, there is a smell.

AFRICAN (OVAMBO)

Who does not tire, succeeds.

PORTUGUESE

Whoever said that money can't buy happiness didn't know where to shop.

AMERICAN

Who lies with dogs rises with fleas.

IRISH

Who loves his work and knows to spare may live and flourish anywhere.

GERMAN

Who serves two kings deceives one of them.

YIDDISH

WHO SPEAKS, SOWS;
WHO LISTENS, REAPS.

ARGENTINE

Who undertakes too much seldom succeeds.

DUTCH

Willful waste makes woeful want.

ENGLISH

Wink at small faults, for you have great ones yourself.

SCOTTISH

Wisdom likes not chance.

ENGLISH

Wishes won't wash dishes.

AMERICAN

With a golden anchor, one can moor in every bay.

GERMAN

With a sweet tongue and kindness, you can drag
an elephant by a hair.

PERSIAN

With lies you will go far, but not back again.

YIDDISH

With money, a dragon; without money, a worm.

CHINESE

Without customers your goods are as worthless as grass.

CHINESE

Without danger, we cannot get beyond danger.

ENGLISH

Without luck, nothing will succeed.

YIDDISH

Woe to him who waits until the last day.

IRISH

Words of gold are often followed by deeds of lead.

DUTCH

Work does not end until your two hands are laid upon your breast.

ESTONIAN

Work fears the resolute man.

CHINESE

Worry, not work, kills man.

MALTESE

Wrinkled purses make wrinkled faces.

ENGLISH

Write like the learned, speak like the masses.

INDIAN (HINDI)

You are as old as you feel.

You are never too old to learn.

You are ushered in according to your dress, shown
out according to your brains.

You can't load a small boat with a heavy cargo.

You can't put "Thank you" in your pocket.
YIDDISH

You can't ride in all directions at the same time.
YIDDISH

You don't know who is your friend or enemy until the ice breaks.
ICELANDIC

You may deal in rags and dress in velvet.
YIDDISH

You may delay, but time will not.
AMERICAN

You never graduate from the school of patience.

RUSSIAN

You never know what you can do until you try.

ENGLISH

You sit at ease when you lend your money; you stand waiting
anxiously when you try to get it back.

KOREAN

Your acquaintance must fill the empire; your close friends
must be few.

CHINESE

Your enemy makes you wise.

ITALIAN

Your goodwill toward others returns to yourself in the end.

JAPANESE